A MÉTIS CHRISTMAS
Thelma's Gift

Written by Julie Coulter Bellon

Illus

This book is dedicated to my grandmother, Thelma Chalifoux, who loved being Métis and worked hard to make sure all Métis have a voice in this world.

A Métis Christmas: Thelma's Gift

Copyright © 2022 Julie Coulter Bellon
Illustration Copyright © 2022 Mikey Brooks

All rights reserved. This book or parts thereof may not be reproduced in any form, stored in any retrieval system, or transmitted in any form by any means—electronic, mechanical, photocopy, recording, or otherwise—without prior written permission of the publisher, except as provided by United States of America copyright law. For permission requests visit www.juliecoulterbellon.com

Paperback Edition
ISBN: 978-1-7363129-3-3

A Note from the Author

The Métis people and culture are unique. They celebrate two heritages—being both First Nations and European. They have a distinctive language called *Michif* that is in danger of being lost. Their beautiful traditions include a form of dancing called jigging and gathering with family to tell the ancestor stories and eat delicious food like *bannock*. This book is intended to introduce children to the Métis language and traditions through Thelma, a Métis girl, and what she experiences.

Thelma was so excited she couldn't help but dance around the house in her favorite moccasins. Tonight was the *Réveillon* celebration and tomorrow would be Christmas! The day was finally here.

Everyone was busy getting ready. There would be lots of food, singing, and jigging. Then presents in the morning. She could hardly wait.

Dancing into the kitchen, Thelma sniffed the air. Her mother was making *bannock* and *rababou* stew. Thelma's mouth watered. *Bannock* and jam were her favorite.

Mama bent down and tucked Thelma's hair behind her ear.
"Do not dance near the stove, *enn fii*," she said.
Mama always called Thelma, "my girl."

Dancing away from the stove into the front room, Thelma did her fancy step and twirled to her grandpa. He sat in his big chair, tuning his fiddle so he could play for the jigging. There was no faster fiddler in the whole world than her *mooshoom*. His eyes twinkled when he picked up his fiddle and played a little tune for her. She did her best shuffle, toe tap, and twirl.

Mooshoom smiled. "Your feet are faster than the fox's today," he told her. She laughed and took a bow before she danced to her parents' room.

Her father wore his best beaded shirt and the colorful sash that Mama had woven for him.

The colors of the people were very important, and he would wear it when he told the ancestor stories tonight. He always told the best stories to remember the loved ones who had once lived, but now watched over and guided them.

Papa leaned down and kissed Thelma on the cheek. "*Ma fii*, you are very grown-up now and you must listen closely when your *Kokum* tells the story of Jesus tonight."

Thelma nodded. She would listen, but she mostly wanted to dance.

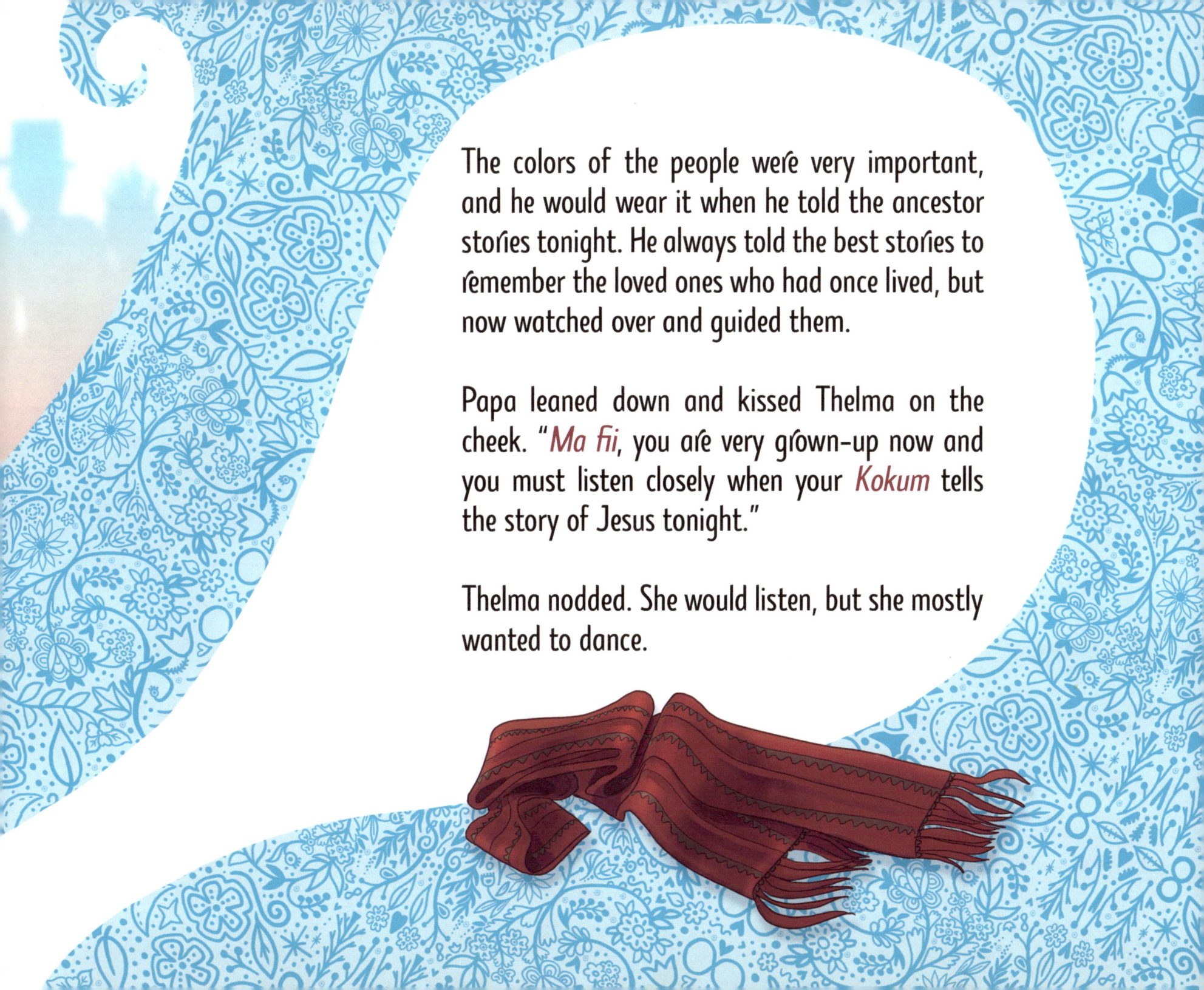

When it was time, *Kokum* gathered everyone close to the fireplace and she sat in the rocking chair that was so old, it creaked as if it wanted to tell the tales of the ancestors. *Kokum* leaned over the big family Bible and read the story of baby Jesus.

Thelma listened close, just as her father asked, but this year, she had questions. When *Kokum* finished and everyone moved to the table to get some food and visit a while, Thelma went to her grandmother's side.

"I have a question, *Kokum*." She climbed in *Kokum's* lap. "When I am happy, all I want to do is jig. Jigging makes everyone happy." She wiggled her toes and the beads on her moccasins sparkled. "Don't you think?"

Her *Kokum* held her close. "Yes, my girl, I feel so happy when I watch you dance."

Thelma wrinkled her nose. "But when you read the story of baby Jesus, no one danced for him." She'd listened very closely. "The shepherds did not dance."

"Perhaps they were tired from walking to find the baby."
Her grandmother winked.

"The angels didn't dance."

Her grandmother nodded.
"Perhaps they didn't know how
and all they could do was sing."

"The wisemen didn't dance."

Kokum squeezed her shoulder. "They brought fine gifts."

Thelma took a deep breath. "When I think about Jesus and what I would do if I'd been in Bethlehem, I would want to dance. To jig my very best jig for him with all the fancy steps."

"Dancing is your gift, my girl. That's how you can show your love for him." She gently nudged Thelma off her lap. "Dance for him."

Her *mooshoom* began to play his fiddle and Thelma's feet slowly tapped with the music. She closed her eyes. The fiddle music flowed over and through her. Thinking about Jesus made her feet go faster.

The love in her heart grew bigger, the more she danced.

Lifting her hands high, she thought of the singing angels, the gift-giving wise men, and the humble shepherds.

They were all in her heart.
In her dance.

The last notes rose to the ceiling and Thelma finished her jig. She bowed before she took *Kokum's* hand. Smiling up at her, she leaned in. "This is the best Christmas ever."

Her *Kokum* patted her cheek. "Never forget your gift for the baby, my girl. And the feeling in your heart when you shared it tonight."

Squeezing *Kokum's* hand, Thelma nodded. Every time she jigged from now on, she would remember when she danced for the Christ child.

And she would feel happy inside.

Glossary of Words

Réveillon—a dinner and celebration held the evening before Christmas.

Rababou stew—a thick soup that includes pemmican or chicken and wild vegetables.

Bannock—a flat round bread.

Enn fii—my girl.

Mooshoom—grandfather.

Kokum—grandmother.

About The Author

Julie Coulter Bellon is the mother of eight children and her favorite time of day is always storytime. She loves reading and telling stories that spark imagination and conversation, especially about her Métis heritage. Julie hopes readers will find an introduction to a culture rich in traditions that they might not have known before, but will come to love. When she is not writing children's books, Julie is an award-winning author of over two dozen romantic suspense novels. You can learn more about Julie and her books at www.juliebellon.com

About The Illustrator

When he's not saving the world from evil villains or changing diapers, Mikey Brooks is teaching art to his 380+ students, writing, illustrating, or daydreaming. He's published ten middle-grade books and several more picture books—a few even won awards! He lives in Utah with his beautiful wife, their six adorable kiddos, a dog named T-Rexie, too many fish to count, and one or two invisible dragons. You can learn more about him at: www.mikeybrooks.com

Printed in the USA
CPSIA information can be obtained
at www.ICGtesting.com
LVHW061017141124

796389LV00004BA/95